An Introduction to
Conducting
Value Studies

A User Guide to Concept Optimization, Problem-Solving, Increased Performance and Value Improvement

Martyn R. Phillips

Certified Value Specialist
Professional Engineer

3rd Edition: April 2015   Modified: July 2017

ISBN-10: 0991737865   ISBN-13: 978-0991737864

Contents: An Introduction to Conducting Value Studies

Compiled by: Value Assurance Resources 360 Inc. Program & Project Advisory Services

Further information may be obtained from:

info@valueassurance.org

Originated in Canada

Who Should Read This Guide

◆ Persons making long-lasting decisions on business and technical issues that will have far-reaching effects

◆ Persons initiating value studies

◆ Persons responsible for value study results

◆ Persons participating in a value study workshop.

Example Benefits

Some of the benefits obtained from well-orchestrated value studies are:

◆ Greater degree of confidence that programs, projects and products will fulfill user needs and meet predicted budgets and schedules

◆ Clearer understanding of risks and potential impacts

◆ Stakeholder acceptance, commitment and "ownership" of proposals

◆ Enhanced designs and reduced design/development time

◆ Managed innovation and optimized life-cycle costs

◆ Re-activated projects following budgetary problems

◆ Smoother program and project implementation

◆ Increased staff awareness of value and risk management goals

◆ Team building and reduced inter organization conflict

◆ Higher return-on-investment of capital and operational outlays

◆ Alignment of strategies, resources, capabilities, processes, technologies and stakeholders

◆ Extremely fast results with outstanding return on effort.

On *"the way things have always been done"*.........

Excerpt from **The Path of the Calf** by Samuel Foss, 1894

One day through the primeval wood,
A calf walked home as good calves should;
But made a trail all bent askew,
A crooked trail as calves all do.

Since then three hundred years have fled,
And, I infer, the calf is dead.
But still he left behind his trail
And thereby hangs my moral tale.

The trail was taken up next day
By a lone dog that passed that way;
And then a wise bellwether sheep
Pursued the trail o'er vale and steep,
And drew the flock behind him too
As good bellwethers always do.

And from that day, o'er hill and glade
Through those old woods a path was made.
And thus, before men were aware,
A city's crowded thoroughfare.
And soon the central street was this,
Of a renowned metropolis.

And men two centuries and a half
Trod in the footsteps of that calf.
Each day a hundred thousand route
Followed this calf about.
And on his crooked journey went
The traffic of a continent.

A hundred thousand men were led
By one calf near three centuries dead.
They followed still his crooked way
And lost one hundred years each day.

For thus such reverence is lent
To well established precedent.

Similarly, we should be aware of the impacts of our own paradigms.

Preface

About this Guide

This guide is based on many years of practical application to a variety of programs and projects worldwide. It provides a good understanding of the value study process and how it is applied to programs and projects. The purpose of this booklet is to outline the essential steps of a typical value study and to enable the consensus-building and decision-making processes for obtaining approvals to proceed further. The focus of this guide applies to "hard" projects and to "soft" projects and problems of business management. More information on the topic of improving performance and value may be obtained in the publications listed at the back of the booklet (**page 38**).

Reason for This Guide

Today, more than ever, there is a complexity of factors to be addressed and, typically, many stakeholders to be consulted when undertaking projects of any size, in any field. Application of the value study process fast-tracks a common understanding of the problems, potential solutions and related implications, together with guiding the consensus-building and decision-making processes.

The value study process has been used for many years. There are several publications on the subject of value improvement. The idea for this short guide grew from recognition that despite the availability of this information, there are many people who do not really understand the basic process. Not all value study participants receive training in value study process prior to participating in workshops. Some of these people resist the process and impede progress of what is a fast-paced, group process. The purpose of this guide is to present a simple explanation of what to expect when initiating or participating in a value study workshop. In this way, valuable staff resources can be maximized and more effective results obtained in far less time.

Preface (Continued)

What This Guide Will Do for You

Persons new to the value study process will quickly gain an insight to what is involved in participating in a study and particularly the value workshop. For "old hands", the guide will act as a convenient *aide-memoire* for the content and order of each step in the value study process. By acquainting all participants of the process and requirements of a value study, maximum effort can be applied to the specific problem (opportunity) under consideration.

Areas of application

Value studies are conducted across a variety of application types in various sectors, as illustrated for example, in **Figure 1**, below. Example project performance issue areas are shown in **Figure 2** (see page x).

Figure 1. Example Application Areas

Preface (Continued)

Some Definitions

There are many varying interpretations of terminology relating to value identification and improvement work. The following selection is useful.

Value takes into account the total cost of ownership as well as compliance with users' requirements, reliability of performance, risk implications, appropriate quality and functionality, along with after-sale support where applicable. Maximum value may be represented by the lowest life cycle cost to reliably accomplish the minimum required performance.

The **Value Methodology** is a systematic process to plan or optimize the value of projects, products or services by providing appropriate functionality to meet the required performance at the lowest overall cost. The Value Methodology is applied within a **value study** comprising pre-workshop, workshop(s) and post workshop activities.

The Value Methodology may be applied as a "quick response" type of study or as a deeply integrated part of an overall organizational desire to stimulate innovation and improve quality. The foundation of the Value Methodology is **function analysis**, which is a special technique for defining a process or project for shared understanding of how it works and where improvement opportunities exist.

Value Analysis (VA), Value Engineering (VE) and Value Management (VM) are applied typically through the use of the Value Methodology.

Value studies are applied to a wide variety of applications, including industrial or consumer products, infrastructure projects, manufacturing processes, business procedures, services, major systems and business plans.

Preface (Continued)

Examples of the varying focus of value studies are identified in **Section 2, Process Overview**.

Value Analysis / Value Engineering is a function based, creative approach used to optimize capital & life-cycle costs, save time, increase profits, improve quality, expand market share, solve problems and / or use resources more effectively.

Value Management is a term that is sometimes synonymous with Value Analysis or Value Engineering. Alternatively, Value Management has also been described as a strategic approach to establish, at the start of a project, the overall concept for subsequent development. This is achieved through the use of workshops at the early stages of a project and is complemented by subsequent application of Value Engineering techniques, while placing emphasis on whole-life costing.

Value Improving Practices (VIPs) are utilized in the process industry. Value Engineering is one of several VIPS, - which are typically applied over a very short timeframe

Value Assurance is an overarching and pro-active approach for ensuring and demonstrating to higher management and other stakeholders that anticipated business returns are being obtained for programs and large projects. It is a holistic process applied as a continuum over the whole program / project life, and it provides both a forward-looking management framework and an ongoing audit trail. For a program of multiple projects, value assurance is ideally accomplished through use of a comprehensive and integrated suite of interactive templates and tools, with smart links to data bases, performance profiles and an overall, multi-attribute, value assurance index. Value assurance generates and continually updates the project value file.

This booklet is a companion to *An Introduction to Value Assurance*, **reference publication 1** (see page 38).

In a Nutshell

What is Value?

Rather like beauty, value can vary with the eye of the beholder (or stakeholder). Value may be measured in "hard" monetary terms, or by an amalgamation of a number of hard and "soft" attributes (measurable qualitatively or quantitatively). The more diverse the stakeholder representation, the more varied the views on what constitutes value.

What is a Value Study?

A value study is a powerful management technique that yields tremendous returns. It is, typically, a multi-disciplinary team process for the identification and testing of optimal solutions. The study is conducted as the establishment, examination and improvement of a defined "base case" (or current state), through a well-established and structured process. A Value Methodology workshop is part of a value study, which in turn, is a key part of a value framework for the effective guidance of development and improvement of a program or project. Note:

1. A value study is not a design or technical review process but is an examination of how to best satisfy stakeholder needs and values in line with the prevailing business case. A value study is a business planning and improvement tool.
2. A value workshop should not be used as just an item on a routine, "check in the box", project administrative process.

Example Value Study Outcomes

- Strategies & master plans for environmental improvement
- Options identification and concept selection /definition for major building, energy and transportation projects
- Cost reduction, schedule and functionality improvements for a variety of major building, energy environmental and transportation projects. Project rescue and re-alignment
- Optimization of operating systems & contracts; re-alignment of corporate growth plans. Risk management plans.

In a Nutshell (Continued)

Value Study Process In a Nutshell

The value study process is routinely described as comprising: Pre-Workshop; Workshop (Information, Analysis, Creativity, Evaluation, Development & Presentation); Post Workshop.

This process is sometimes misrepresented and shortened, leading to sub-optimal results. Experience shows that the degree of overall success and acceptance of the results of a value study is directly proportional to the planning, control and follow-through efforts invested in it. This requires attention to the following key points. **Page 26** provides a milestones checklist.

■ **Initiation and Establishing a Framework Success**
- Ensure clarity of purpose; quantify objectives; develop plan
- Identify and commit adequate, multi-disciplinary resources, including senior, 3rd party specialists
- Brief re. expectations in sufficient time

■ **Creating the Conditions for Success**
- Define the "base case" (current way of operation or design)
- Relate to business case requirements
- Assess performance of the base case
- Compile workshop <u>input</u> text and summary presentations

■ **Conducting the Innovation Workshop(s) Effectively**
- Brief all team members on the workshop process
- Target function improvement opportunities
- Conduct the innovation and testing process
- Compare options and consolidate interim outputs

■ **Incorporating the Changes & Ensuring Effective Outcomes**
- Collate details of ideas and related cost & schedule impacts
- Prepare workshop record, management overview & <u>output</u> presentation. Verify technical & financial viability of ideas
- Develop draft recommendations; hold decision meeting
- Confirm stakeholder acceptance, develop change plan
- Formally close study; monitor incorporation and implementation of proposals.

Contents

Figure 2. Example Project Performance Issue Areas

> **Note.** Health and safety, etc., are not shown as
> performance issue areas as they are generally
> treated as "go - no go" (i.e. pass / fail) aspects

1. Introduction

Why Conduct Value Studies?

Anyone who is required to direct, plan and control an investment in resources, to meet time, cost and quality parameters, will benefit from reading this guide. A value study assists in providing clear project direction, significantly reduced development and decision-making time, together with balancing life-cycle impacts and minimizing project risks. This also directly enhances teamwork and communication, together with increasing stakeholder satisfaction, consensus and maximizing return on investment.

Value studies assist in developing a competitive edge for a wide range of private sector and public service business programs. Increasingly the value process is being accepted as a very effective tool for ensuring best value for money, while in no way compromising quality. A value study is a function-based technique that identifies key areas to improve quality, streamline tasks and reduce whole-life costs. The degree of savings and functional enhancement increases significantly with the duration and intensity of study effort. Appropriate application of the process provides a multi-disciplinary framework within which to focus team efforts and to subsequently re-focus for on-time, on-budget completion, to stakeholder expected requirements of scope, quality and functionality.

A value study should not be viewed as yet another additional item to be checked on the project manager's imposed "to do" list. Value studies address the traditional, linear development aspects of a project in a remarkably short timeframe. Inter organization barriers are broken down and a common understanding of needs, constraints and values is established, as multi-functional team members address issues together, - at the same time and in the same setting. All stakeholders become heard, while planners and designers are given the opportunity to perform even better and arrive at a mutually acceptable solution sooner, rather than later.

1. Introduction (Continued)

Context of Application

Value studies are the means by which value analysis, value engineering and value management are carried out. To some jurisdictions, the terms value analysis, value engineering and value management are synonymous. One alternative view is to separate value analysis as the rearward looking process that evaluates the current situation or base case. Value engineering is then the creative and testing process for improving that previously analyzed base case. Similarly, there is no universally agreed distinction between value engineering and value management, but there are jurisdictional preferences regarding the terminology and placing differing degrees of emphasis on some of the study phases. A distinction between the two terms tends to be that value management applies to the "softer" upfront, relatively qualitative, applications to business management, strategic planning, needs assessment and concept definition. By the same token, value engineering may be seen as application of the value study process to the "harder", quantitative applications of concept development and design.

The common thread running throughout all of these interpretations is the use of the Value Methodology (VM) as the guiding process by which to conduct value studies. The process originated as value analysis in the mid-1940s at a major US manufacturing company. The name changed from Value analysis to value engineering in the 1950s and then, in the UK in the 1960s to value management. Eventually the term Value Methodology was adopted in the US, but the terms value analysis, value engineering and value management are still used, somewhat interchangeably across the globe.

A key difference between the Value Methodology and other management / problem-solving approaches is the use of function analysis (FA). The Value Methodology requires stringent use of FA although there are some jurisdictions that still do not employ this influential, enabling tool.

2. Process Overview

Application

Value studies are applicable to both "hard and "soft" projects at different stages of development. Examples of changing study focus are listed below and described further in **Table 1**.

Strategic Direction
◆ **V1, Value Management** - to determine options for clear, unambiguous and workable business strategies prior to formal commitment to develop program(s) and projects

Concept Definition
◆ **V2, Value Analysis** - to ensure optimum functionality and cost effectiveness; to confirm/modify realistic budget

Project Development & Execution
◆ **V3**, **Value Engineering** - to "tighten" project proposals and ensure maximum cost efficiency within the allocated budget

In-Service Optimization
◆ **V4, Value Control** - to analyze and optimize an in-service process or facility.

Value Optimization Program

It is preferable that a value study is not conducted in isolation from other review practices within an organization. Also the results of a value study will be more effective if the process and follow-through are visibly supported by senior management. A value policy along with related procedures are helpful with this.

As well, a value study should be undertaken within the purview of an overall value optimization program that a) ensures follow-through of agreed study recommendations, and, b) has specific performance parameters and measures for tracking of program effectiveness. A comprehensive program will also address aspects of a project value management plan, value engineering change proposals (VECPs), interfaces with other related initiatives such as risk management and staff training.

2. Process Overview (Cont.d)

Focus of Application	Example of Required Outcomes
I. Business Program Alignment / Strategic Direction	
V1. Needs Analysis & Scoping **V1. Strategic Planning**	Agreed stakeholder needs and definition of program / project scope. Consensus development on stakeholders' key issues and potential scenarios. Agreed, tested and unambiguous business strategies, criteria & clear implications prior to start of asset planning & design. Business risks identification and mitigation strategy. Master plan.
II. Concept Definition	
V2. Concept/ Feasibility **V2. Functional Design**	"Menu" of project(s) options, relative cost-benefits, performance standards, affordability, potential risk areas, liabilities, uncertainties & sensitivities (to data accuracy, projections, etc.).. Consensus and confirmation of best value outline design, phasing and strategies for implementation, contracting & risk management.
III. Project Development & Execution	
V3. Detailed Design **V3. Contract / Sub contract Awards**	Implementation/constructability improvement together with elimination of unnecessary cost, while maintaining or enhancing functionality Verification of project requirements and capability to perform as specified. Rescue of an "over-budget" and/or behind schedule project; creation and analysis of alternative proposals
IV. In Service Optimization	
V4. In Service Program Optimization & Turnaround	Post occupancy review and project enhancements Analysis and improvement of operational performance. Completion of feedback loop to strategic planning process as part of an overall "expert" system and continuous improvement

Table 1. Range of Application of Value Studies

2. Process Overview (Cont.d)

Value Study Outline

The following sections describe the basics of a formal value study process. These basics apply to all such studies, regardless of the application and stage of development of the program or project. There is a vast array of value improvement tools (described in other publications) that are applied within this process. Focusing on essential function requirements and stakeholder ideals is of paramount importance in all values studies.

The overall scope of a value study comprises specific stages and steps. Each stage and associated step is a requisite foundation of the next. A value study work plan is required.

■ *Pre-Workshop.* Initiation, mandate, planning and logistics. Pre-workshop information gathering, sifting and analysis, to ensure an efficient start to the workshop. In line with the fundamentals of good project management, it is necessary at the outset to ensure absolute clarity of stakeholder expectations, project definition, required deliverables and team commitments.

■ *Workshop.* Workshop(s), conducted in six distinct phases. A workshop detailed agenda should be followed, with no deviation from process and timings, such that maximum team efficiency is derived. The workshop is the heart of a value study process and requires progress through the steps in a clear, linear sequence. It also encourages iteration back to previous steps, as required, for clarification, improvement of thinking, refinement of decision-making data and consensus development.

■ *Post Workshop.* Post workshop confirmation, completion and refinement of workshop outputs. Reporting and follow-up tasks, followed by formal acceptance/ rejection of specific proposals.

Stakeholder consensus-building is accomplished throughout the value study process. It is important that the results of a value study are validated, approved and then truly embedded in the subsequent project development phases, such that the planned degree of value improvement is actually attained.

3. Value Study Proceedings

Group Process

A value study is a group problem (or opportunity) resolution process. It is conducted through a single workshop study, or series of workshops, with defined expectations and beginning / end points. The power of the value study lies in the structured sequence of activities, team synergy and ongoing consensus development. This is achieved through the workshop process. To gain maximum benefit, the temptation to change the sequence of activities or to short circuit the workshop process must be avoided. A further pitfall to be avoided is that of proceeding in isolation (i.e. on an individual basis) or in treating the whole process as a series of traditionally conducted meetings.

The stages and steps of a value study are illustrated in **Figure 3**. The workshop forms just part of the overall process. Ideally the six workshop phases are conducted within one, continuous session, depending on the type, timing and aims of the workshop. However, strategic value studies may be spread over a number of weeks and separate workshops. Relative emphasis and timings for the phases vary with the progress of the program/project.

Study Participants

All participants should be carefully selected and then familiarized with the study & workshop process, so that progress will not be disrupted by relative newcomers holding rigidly to their old paradigms and values. Study participants include a (small) steering group, a (small) planning group, a workshop core group and, as may be necessary, peripheral, designated workshop team support members. Collectively, the study participants should represent a broad cross-section of the project stakeholders, at varying levels of seniority. Roles should be clear. Experience shows that value workshops run more smoothly and productively if the majority of participants have received value training. It is important to identify a corporate champion of the value optimization program and a sponsor of a particular value study.

3. **Value Study Proceedings** (Cont.d)

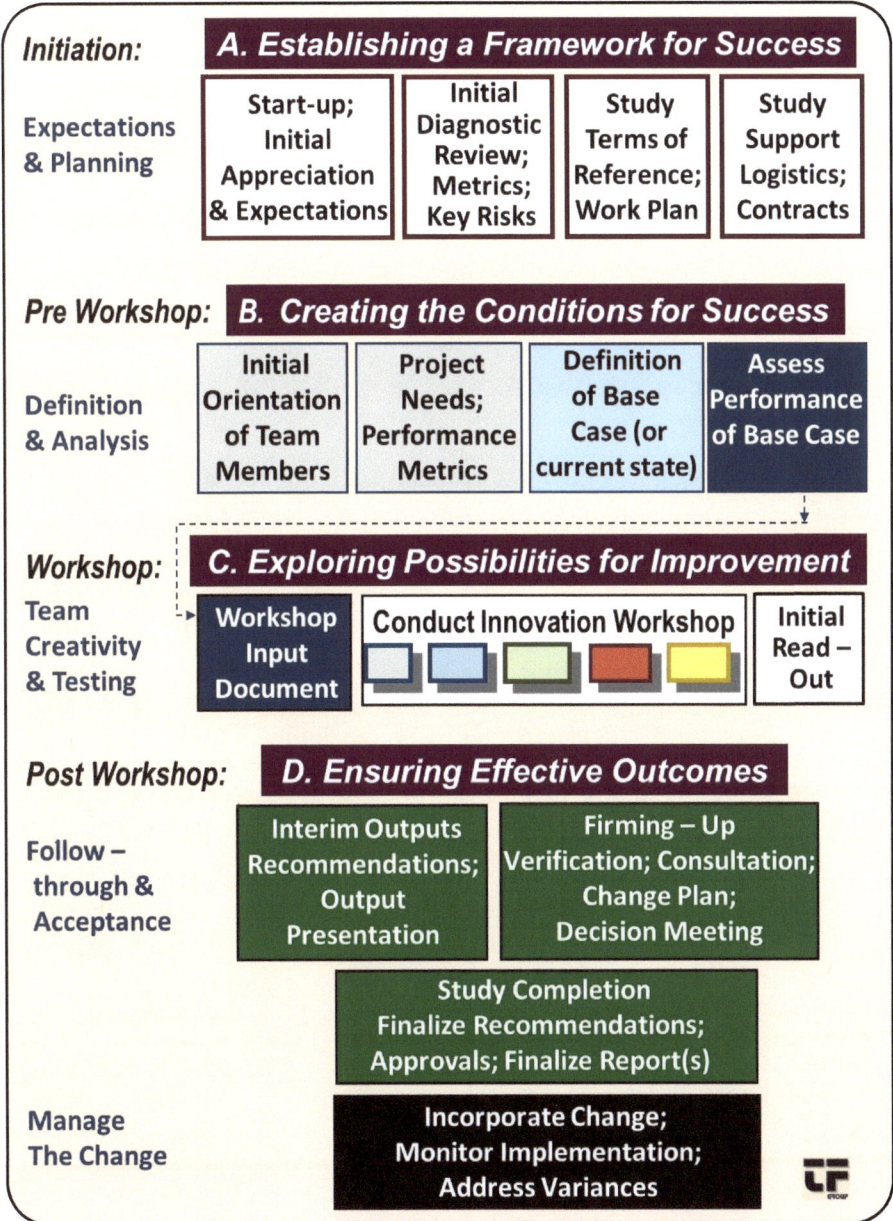

Initiation: | **A. *Establishing a Framework for Success***

Expectations & Planning

| Start-up; Initial Appreciation & Expectations | Initial Diagnostic Review; Metrics; Key Risks | Study Terms of Reference; Work Plan | Study Support Logistics; Contracts |

Pre Workshop: | **B. *Creating the Conditions for Success***

Definition & Analysis

| Initial Orientation of Team Members | Project Needs; Performance Metrics | Definition of Base Case (or current state) | Assess Performance of Base Case |

Workshop: | **C. *Exploring Possibilities for Improvement***

Team Creativity & Testing

| Workshop Input Document | Conduct Innovation Workshop | Initial Read – Out |

Post Workshop: | **D. *Ensuring Effective Outcomes***

Follow – through & Acceptance

| Interim Outputs Recommendations; Output Presentation | Firming – Up Verification; Consultation; Change Plan; Decision Meeting |

Study Completion
Finalize Recommendations; Approvals; Finalize Report(s)

Manage The Change

Incorporate Change; Monitor Implementation; Address Variances

Figure 3.   Value Study Stage & Steps

3. Value Study Proceedings (Cont.d)

The following is a useful additional set of categories against which to check that proper representation of stakeholders will be at the workshop or included in the planning and review groups.

- ☑ Owner(s) of the problem/opportunity
- ☑ Those responsible for resolution
- ☑ Those responsible for implementation & operation
- ☑ Those impacted by the solution(s): a) externally during installation / construction, b) externally during routine operation, c) user group(s)
- ☑ Facilitator (who focuses on guiding the study process)
- ☑ Cost, schedule, administrative & technical support.

As projects have become larger and more complex, with a trend to develop consensus among a wider range of stakeholders, it is becoming commonplace to have larger workshop teams. Ideally the workshop team should be as small as possible, with a mechanism for communicating to the broader stakeholder base outside the main workshop. Large, complex projects and large stakeholder groups benefit from a multi-step study approach: 18 specific steps with 100+ activities. The workshop is only a part.

Shown below are some additional aspects of team composition:

- Multi-disciplinary: financial & range of technical
- Multiple viewpoints: Owner, funding agency, user, planner, designer, constructor, facility manager, regulator, environmentalist, constructive challenger(s)
- Lateral thinkers, open minded, listeners
- Contributors to group thinking process
- Positive attitude toward to value methodology
- Relevant project and VM experience
- Diversity of participation (young to mature, etc.)
- Not all related to the original design
- Person(s) to represent the "voice of the customer".

3. Value Study Proceedings (Cont.d)

Indication of Time Requirements

Viewpoints vary on how much time should be allocated to conduct an effective value study. The following allocation has worked well for a variety of value studies conducted for different applications around the world. Notwithstanding, study timeframes can be compressed for urgent situations, or on the other hand, expanded to suit availability of team and information.

***Value Study Stage A:* Pre-Workshop**   *Approx. Timing*

- Initiation and Scoping; Initial Diagnostic Review   *Week -2*
    - Value Statement, Key Issues and Risks
    - Performance Profiles & Value Index
- Workshop, Team & Equipment Logistics
- Definition of Base Case – Descriptions & Cost Models
- Site / Data Familiarization; Initial Function Analysis
- Benchmarking; Value Comparisons; Value Gap
- Briefing Package Preparation; Team Review   *Week -1*
- Preparation for Workshop Input Presentations
- Team VM Process Orientation

***Value Study Stage B:* Workshop** (2 – 4 days duration) *Week 1*

- Summary Review of Information (Input Presentations)
- Function and Issues Analysis / Review
- Initial Creativity
- Preliminary Evaluation / Ideas Screening & Extension
- Outline Development of Value Enhancement Proposals (VEPs)
- Comparison, Selection and Consolidation of Most Likely VEPs
- Read-out / Informal Presentation & Interim Output Summary

***Value Study Stage C:* Post Workshop**

- Collation & Fine-tuning of Workshop Outputs   *Week 2*
- Risks Review; Development of *Draft* Overview Report
- Verification / Extension / Completion / Summaries of VEPs
- Initial Decision Meeting; Broaden Consultation
- Formal Report, Presentation & Recommendations *Week 3*
- Approvals, Implementation, Monitoring Study Close-Out.

Value study key activities are illustrated in **Fig. 4**. & the **Appendix.**

3. Value Study Proceedings (Cont.d)

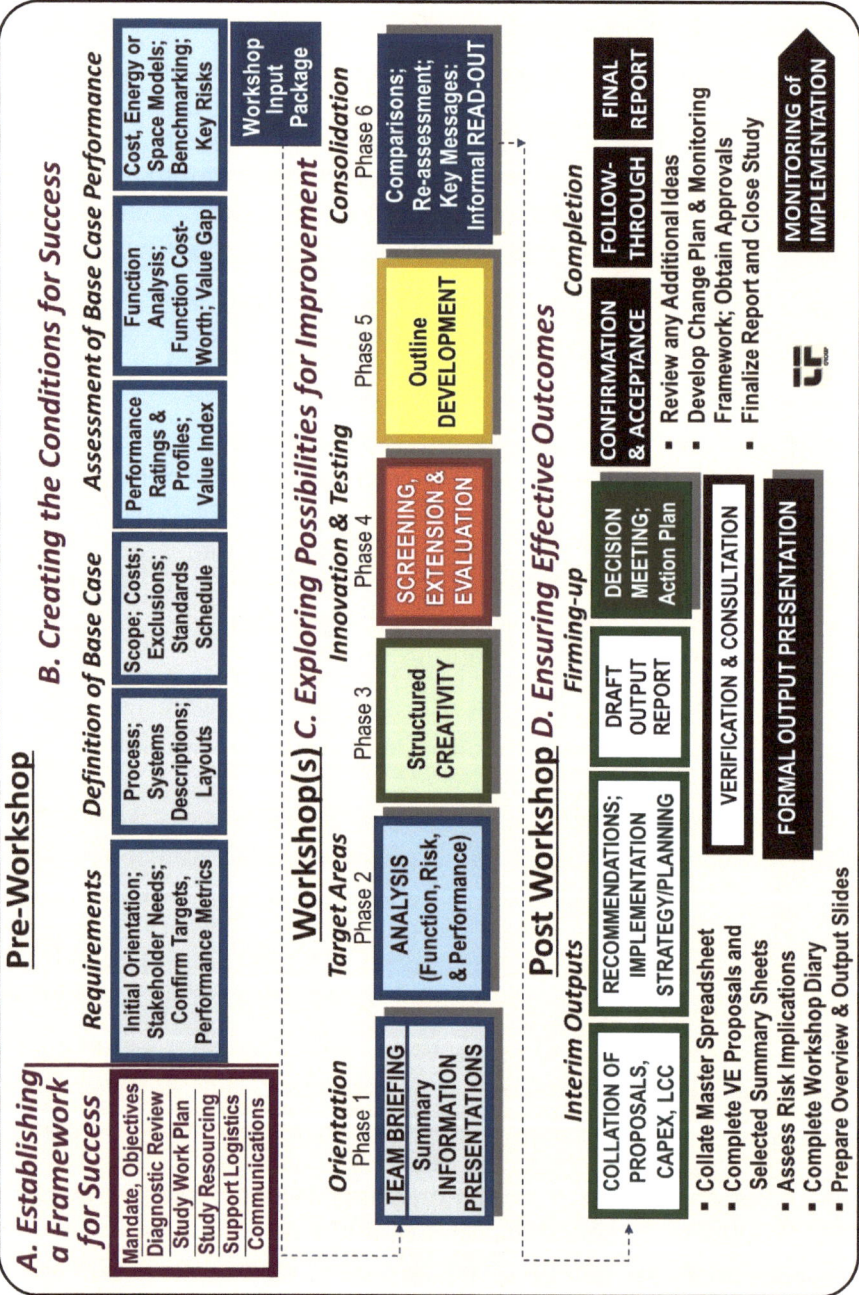

Figure 4   Value Study Activities

3. Value Study Proceedings (Cont.d)

Facilitation Aims

Facilitation of both the workshop activities and the overall study process is required.   In particular, the following facets must be carefully addresses throughout:

> ➢ **Purpose Facet:** to consider project & stakeholder requirements
> ➢ **Project Facet:** to determine and achieve stakeholder agreed outcomes within the constraints imposed
> ➢ **People Facet:** to deal with variety of attitudes, build consensus and ensure group congruence
> ➢ **Process Facet:** to diffuse communication barriers, align focus and document the process transparently.

Facilitation of the workshop is best accomplished by a person external to the problem/opportunity under consideration.   In this way, inherent biases can be pre-empted and objective results ensured.

Golden Rules

#1 Never short-circuit the process, no matter how tempted or rushed you are, or your client is. Instead lower expectations of scope, or stage the work to what can be managed comfortably and rigorously.

#2 Ensure proper pre-workshop preparation is conducted

#3 "Think function": <u>What</u> must be achieved and <u>why</u>? This approach opens up a vast array of possibilities for exploring alternatives for <u>how</u> to achieve the objective(s).

#4 Discourage team members from only partial attendance at workshops. If some individuals are too busy to attend full-time, they will likely upset the workshop dynamics. So, a) they should not attend at all (they will disrupt proceedings), b) they might serve a better purpose by being part of the steering/review group and attend the starting & finishing presentations

#5   Allow time for clarification, refinement and confirmation.

4. Preparation for Workshop

Focus: *Expectations & Requirements*

Initiation, Needs and Assessment Metrics

Prior to launching into a workshop, it is critical to garner stakeholder expectations and requirements for success of the program or project under study, along with setting parameters for the value study and workshop success. An initial **diagnostic review** session should be undertaken (at a senior level) prior to undertaking any value workshop. This should consider:

- Problem/opportunity definition
- Business case requirements
- Value proposition and desired outcomes
- Value drivers and performance metrics
- Key risk areas, constraints and study no-go areas
- Key target improvement areas
- Mandate, objectives & targets.

Initiation of the workshop requires sufficient time and attention to:

- Value team membership and roles [including "cold eye(s)"]
- Coordinating arrangements for participants
- Logistics - venue, equipment, timetable for implementation, verification, consultation and approval
- Information gathering and assessment; team briefing
- clear understanding and succinct documentation of the "base case" definition and assessment of its current performance.

Key Questions

- What is the problem (opportunity) to be resolved?
- Why is it a problem (opportunity)?
- When is resolution required?
- What would be the outcome(s) of NOT resolving it?
- Who is responsible for resolution and follow-through?

➲ **Output: Value study directive and work plan**

4. Preparation for Workshop (Cont.d)

Base Case Definition

Part of the preparatory work involves clear definition of the "Base Case" (i.e. the way the system works now or the current design).

Actions:

- ☐ Describe Base Case (existing way)
- ☐ Develop outline systems descriptions
- ☐ Provide simplified key diagrams
- ☐ Review
  - ➢ Design premise and operational needs
  - ➢ Governing standards
  - ➢ Contractual arrangements & communications
  - ➢ Benchmarking (costs, schedule, functionality)
  - ➢ Alternatives considered & reasons for rejection
  - ➢ Range of operating conditions
  - ➢ Sparing arrangements
  - ➢ Reliability, availability & service level/class
  - ➢ Special requirements & sensitivities
- ☐ Develop CAPEX, OPEX, LCC, energy and space models
- ☐ Define overall project budget and schedule milestones.

➥ **Output: Information Summary Package**

Base Case Analysis

Traditionally, the Value Methodology "job plan" requires analysis of the base case to be conducted during Phase 2 of the workshop. However, practicalities prove that for many applications it is preferable for a workshop planning group to analyze the Base Case (or current state) in advance of the workshop and present the findings to the whole team at the beginning of the workshop.

4. Preparation for Workshop (Cont.d)

Within the traditional Value Methodology, **function analysis (FA)** is a critical activity. This is what sets the Value methodology apart from other management techniques. A useful aspect of function analysis is a function-logic [Function Analysis System Technique (FAST)] diagram; especially so when annotated with the cost of functions and other key information (e.g. durations or losses). In addition to FA, there is a number of other analyses that need to be performed prior to the workshop.

Actions:

- ☐ Analyze Project Base Case
  - ➢ Function analysis (active verb- measurable noun)
  - ➢ Basic function and higher order function
  - ➢ Develop FAST diagram
  - ➢ Assign costs to functions *
  - ➢ Benchmark overall worth
  - ➢ Identify value mis-matches
  - ➢ Analyze schedule durations
  - ➢ Identify & analyze key risks / uncertainties
  - ➢ Develop initial performance profiles *
  - ➢ Develop initial (multi-attribute) value index *

Through study planning group and sponsor:

- ☐ Identify data gaps, assumptions, uncertainties & unknowns; areas of difficulty
- ☐ Confirm common understanding of key issues
- ☐ Confirm improvement targets

➲ **Output: Annotated FAST diagram, key risks profile, performance profiles, value index.**

** Traditionally, value is improved by increasing functionality and/or reducing cost. The more effective multi-attribute index is recommended; this method is described in **reference** 2 (Page 38).*

4. Preparation for Workshop (Cont.d)

Input Presentation Package

The foregoing preparatory activities culminate in the development of a summary information, input package. This package can form the first part of the study output report. Ideally the input package is distributed to all workshop team members in advance, as essential pre-workshop reading. Contents, typically in presentation slide (simple) format, should address:

Section 1. Value Study Mandate & Approach

To define management's expectations and the process for achieving them. Project background.

Section 2. Project Requirements

To define management's expectations and the process for achieving them. Project background.

Section 3. Workshop Base Case

To define the overall "Base Case" to be improved.

- **Systems Overviews**
  To describe the systems as proposed for the Base. Case, related issue areas and rejected approaches
- **Project Controls**
  To clarify cost, schedule, milestones, interfacing, PM, procurement & contractual key aspects. Contingencies & sparing
- **Function-Cost Analysis**
  To consider the project by functional breakdown; to apply costs to functions (and systems) rather than by discipline or trade
- **Performance Profiles & Value Index**
  To review presently assessed project performance against agreed parameters and derive initial Value Index
- **Benchmarking of Key Aspects**
  To compare the worth of what is being proposed against other methods used elsewhere to attain similar functionality and cost-efficiency.

5. Workshop Phase
Information

Focus: *Summary review of the Input Presentation package (objective thinking)*

Objectives of This Phase

- To enable all participants to share a common representation of the situation and to appreciate the same "big picture"
- To <u>quickly</u> apprise all workshop team members of information and requirements concerning the current situation or process/design presently proposed.

Present / Receive Information

Key team members to provide short, succinct, overviews of the situation from their perspectives, as per the pre-workshop information package. Presentations should cover: the following categories, split between the knowledgeable representatives of the example areas shown.

Needs Definition

- Funding organization(s)
- Project proponent(s)
- Regulatory agencies
- End-users
- Operator(s)
- Maintenance organization.

Description and Analysis of the Base Case

- Project manager
- Planner(s)
- Designers / Leads
  - Process; Mechanical
  - Electrical; Geotechnical
  - Municipal; Landscape; etc.
- Supplier(s)
- Contractor(s)
- Cost analyst(s)
- "Cold eye(s)" re. observations.

6. Workshop Phase 2
Analysis

Focus: *Review and confirmation of the "Base Case" functions, key issues, value gap & targets (analytical thinking)*

Objectives of This Phase

- To understand completely the specific use or functional requirements of the item, project or system
- To ensure clarity of definition of objectives, issues & risks
- To assimilate and integrate the available information to produce a systematic framework of facts and interrelationships
- To focus subsequent discussions and identify project opportunity areas for the following Creativity phase.

Focus on Functions

Function analysis by is very powerful and sets the overall framework. Develop FAST diagram(s)* to represent the project breakdown for further review. Deepen understanding of the problem (or opportunity). Establish boundaries of the issues to be resolved; highlight logic gaps. Arrange functions in why/how format and develop a project "map". Define key issues & risks.

Function is defined by an <u>active verb</u> plus a <u>measurable noun</u>. Functions are generally listed as follows:

Needs / Objectives ⟸ **WHY?**   **FUNCTIONS**   **HOW?** ⟹ *Managerial*
"Bigger" Picture   */ Technical Solutions*

* FAST diagramming is described fully in References 6 & 7, page 38.

Techniques

- Challenge assumptions, preferences, standards & trends
- Define and evaluate the functions
- Refine FAST model (or Focus diagram)
- Check functions for obvious omissions
- Refine function-cost models; identify function-cost
- Review performance profiles and Value Index.

➲ **Output: Target areas of opportunity to improve value.**

7. Workshop Phase 3
Creativity

Focus: *Initial creativity (divergent thinking)*

Objective of This Phase

To generate a large number of alternatives which could provide the basic function(s), avoiding judgement of their practicality.

Key Question

What else will do the job (i.e. perform the basic functions)?

Generate Alternatives

Brainstorm all conceivable options to meet required functions. Also, give consideration for how to deal with any key risk issues. Use any other forms of creative thinking as appropriate.

Techniques

- Use creative thinking (individual & group brainstorming)
- Don't let regulation, seniority or people control thinking
- Ignore old paradigms; think "outside the box"
- Ignore apparent constraints
- Eliminate, reduce, substitute, adapt
- Try everything imaginable; generate <u>many</u> ideas
- Use checklists
- Over-simplify; blast
- Think conceptually; look for ideas, not solid solutions
- Modify and/or combine alternatives
- Quantity, not quality of ideas
- Hitchhike/piggyback on ideas of others
- No negative attitudes; do *not* criticize
- Freewheel, no barriers; encourage wild ideas
- Suspend judgement; do *not* evaluate.

➲ **Output: List of unjudged creative ideas.**

8. Workshop Phase 4
Evaluation

Focus: *Screening / coarse evaluation of creative ideas (start of convergent thinking)*

Objectives of This Phase

- To determine alternatives which offer appropriate quality/service and the greatest potential for cost/time savings, while increasing value and overall stakeholder satisfaction
- To evaluate, critique & rank alternatives for passing to the next phase, Development.

Key Questions

- Will each alternative perform the required basic function?
- Can it be implemented in time and with little disruption?

Evaluate Alternatives

Use agreed screening criteria to make initial judgements and formulate a preliminary matrix of likely options for further consideration. Identify team members willing to champion ideas.

Activities

- Initial sift to reject 'non-starters' (but don't be too hasty)
- Use "gut feel" judgement, supplement with expert opinion
- Put approximate $ value on each idea
- Evaluate by comparison with ideas in use elsewhere
- Modify / refine /extend ideas
- "Ball park" benefit-cost; consider life cycle impacts.

Note. Voting on merits / rating of the ideas is to be discouraged.

➲ **Output: Sorted list of screened ideas warrant subsequent, quality time for expansion into reliable propositions (value enhancement proposals, VEPs).**

9. Workshop Phase 5
Development

Focus: *Development and testing of screened ideas*

Objectives of This Phase

- To identify likely alternatives(s)
- To obtain firm, convincing information
- To develop written proposals (VEPs)
- To formulate a plan for implementation.

Develop Proposals

Develop and challenge the likely options in terms of: capital cost; life cycle cost; risk areas; implementation schedule; constructability and serviceability. Document advantages, disadvantages and data sources; add calculations, sketches, literature, written descriptions.

Activities

- Work on specifics, not generalities
- Provide convincing logic
- Confirm proposals meet functional requirements
- Confirm standards & targets are achievable/affordable
- Prepare value enhancement proposal (VEP)summary
- Identify life cycle impacts (not just monetary costs)
- Compile data package comparing proposed course of action with baseline case. Provide information sources
- Ensure ALL value criteria will be met
- Identify barriers to implementation.
- Identify impacts on others, scheduling, re-design implications and implementation responsibility.

Life Cycle Costing

An indication of lifecycle cost (LCC) implications should be identified. Derive full LCC if capital costs of competing options are close or if the decision-making process requires this. If complex, seek specialist help between the workshop and review stages.

➲ **Output: A set of clearly documented and well-reasoned, outline proposals (VEPs) for improving project value.**

10. Workshop Phase 6
Consolidation

Focus: *Convergence toward interim outputs for the workshop*

Objectives of This Phase

- To review workshop proposals and group in order of preference for acceptance and follow-up. To refine developed ideas, costs and impacts.
- To consolidate emerging best developed ideas and compare strategies/ scenarios/ options. To apply sensitivity criteria to the emerging outcomes and to identify the "Preferred Option"
- To prepare an integrated implementation plan for the most likely-to-be-accepted value enhancement proposals
- To revise value and risk profiles; determine revised value index or performance improvement factor.

Activities

- Review and collate Value Enhancement Proposal packages technically and financially
- Revise FAST diagram
- Weigh risks of proposals
- Refine & consolidate proposals
- Revise value profile & index
- Compile summary output tables
- Develop decision matrix
- Relate to the business case
- Develop management action plan (general and for each value enhancement proposal)
- Compute cost & time savings; revise models
- Compile key messages
- Prepare interim read-out slides.

Note. SAVE International's Value Methodology shows this phase as the Presentation phase. However for large and complex projects, this is typically too soon. See next pages for the best procedure.

➥ **Output: Workshop interim outputs read-out & feedback.**

10. Workshop Phase 6
Consolidation (Cont.d)

Interim Output Presentation (Read-Out)

Using PowerPoint slides and content from the workshop proceedings, the informal presentation (preferably in the same setting as the workshop) includes the following:

- Brief description and cost breakdown of Base Case, along with schedule milestone dates
- Summary of Base Case problems (high cost, temporary arrangements, difficult construction, risk areas, etc.)
- Results of function analysis / FAST diagramming
- Rationale for selecting and weighting decision criteria
- Technical / cost data supporting selection of the alternative(s)
- Advantages and disadvantages of accepting alternative(s)
- Comparative life cycle impacts
- Clear sketches of before and after outline designs
- Problems, residual issues &associated new risks; cost of implementation or mitigation
- Estimated cost savings, economic and other benefits
- Summary statement & description of implementation milestones
- Trade-offs & roadblocks
- Roles, responsibilities and deadlines for follow- through work.

Considerations: The audience is:

- interested in performance first, with relative advantages and disadvantages of each idea
- influenced by the effect that adoption of the proposal will have on their own particular sphere of work or interest.

The read-out should be punctual, succinct and upbeat. Allow adequate time for receipt of feedback from the Review Panel. Acknowledge feedback and avoid defensiveness by presenters.

11. Post Workshop Outputs

Focus: *Refinement of workshop outputs for presentation, consultation, approval & subsequent implementation.*

Objectives of This Phase

- To complete and refine tasks outstanding from the workshop
- To enable implementation of approved recommendations and formally close the value study.

Activities

- Incorporate responses to Review Panel feedback
- Refine VEPs and master spreadsheet of costs
- Compile formal VEP summaries, as appropriate
- Consider new ideas and proposals submitted
- Verify workshop technical and financial outputs
- Prepare formal output presentation
- Complete Workshop Diary, develop formal output presentation and compile Executive Summary and/or value study Management Overview
- Present formally to senior management and obtain feedback. Speak "the language of the boardroom"
- To conduct stakeholder communication/consultation and obtain endorsements & approval to implement
- Hold formal decision-making meeting and identify responsibilities for follow-through
- Incorporate approved recommendations in Design/Contracts
- Prepare change management and action / monitoring plan; brief and/or train users
- Determine return-on-investment for value study effort
- Compile "lessons learned" and feed into value study program guidelines for future use
- ➲ **Output:** Interim & final study outputs, follow-through activities and record of value study proceedings.

12. Output Documentation

Purpose: *To provide a record of the Value Study proceedings*

Value Study Output Documentation

Value study documentation has a variety of audiences, e.g.:

- Study participants
- Approval authorities and financiers
- Implementers, users
- External stakeholders
- Media.

Therefore, different types of reporting are often required.

Example output documentation is listed below:

- ⮊ Executive presentation and short summary report
- ⮊ Main report (& presentation) for general distribution
  - ❑ Volume 1, Management Overview
- ⮊ Back-up Documentation
  - ❑ Volume 2, Value Study Proposals
  - ❑ Volume 3, Workshop Diary.

Typical contents of an Overview report are listed as follows.

Output Report Table of Contents

Preface (including CVS Facilitator Seal & Signature)

Executive summary

1.0 Introduction
- 1.1 Project Background and Purpose
- 1.2 Project Statistics, Requirements & Performance Metrics
- 1.3 Workshop Mandate and Process
- 1.4 Stakeholders & Value Improvement Opportunity

2.0 Description of the Project Base Case
- 2.1 Overview of the Base Case
- 2.2 Systems Requirements & Descriptions
- 2.3 Scheduling, Contractual & Interfacing Aspects

12. Output Documentation
(Continued)

Output Report Table of Contents (Continued)

13. Study Milestones Checklist

1. Establish mandate: clear, unambiguous, agreed, measurable
2. Ensure proper definition of problem and /or opportunity
3. Establish expectations & schedule of deliverables
4. Conduct diagnostic review; compile value study work plan
5. Identify participants & availabilities:
   - ❑ Steering Group (SG)
   - ❑ Core Group (CG)
   - ❑ Workshop participants - managers, specialists, challenger(s)
   - ❑ Value Team leader (VTL)
   - ❑ Cost coordinator(s) (CAPEX & LCC) & support
   - ❑ Support (administrative & technical) - dedicated
   - ❑ Consultation group(s) and user(s)
6. Arrange logistics e.g. Venue(s), equipment, site visits, etc.
7. Conduct diagnostic analyses (function, cost, space, energy, time, condition, benchmarking, profiles, value index)
8. Issue invitations, joining instructions & briefing document
9. Arrange for attendance by senior management at input and interim output presentations
10. Arrange for Steering Group (SG) Progress Meetings
11. Prepare Input Document & obtain SG approval
12. Issue input document to workshop participants (1 week ahead of site visit and workshop)
13. Brief workshop support personnel re. Expectations of duties, timings, deliverables, formats & filing protocol
14. Check venue signage, workroom layout and adequacy of equipment
15. Ensure receipt of input presentations and integrate
16. Brief presenters, again, immediately before workshop presentation
17. Conduct workshop; ensure no slippage of daily deliverables
18. Review progress with SG representatives
19. Ensure no potentially viable ideas become lost
20. Ensure development sheets are filled-in properly, checked

13. **Study Milestones Checklist** (Continued)

       for quality, tracked for completion and scanned & retained by the recorder

21. Update function & cost models. Revise performance profiles, value index and schedule
22. Review responses to any new risk and residual issues
23. Complete master spreadsheet of proposals & impacts
24. Ensure timely preparation of interim presentation
25. Develop presentation plan and rehearse
26. Issue output presentation handouts to presenters
27. Record feedback to interim output presentation
28. Ensure adequacy/consistency/continuity of workshop records: hard copy and electronic files / directories
29. Check deliverables (as stated before pre-workshop)
30. Issue copies of presentation, feedback and draft executive summary within 1 working day of presentation
31. Issue draft overview report to team members within 3 working days of presentation
32. Ensure proposal summaries are completed; review
33. Ensure timely completion of appendices / support documentation
34. Ensure completion timely of outstanding workshop tasks: verification & fine-tuning of most likely to be acceptable proposals, costing, scheduling and outline specifications
35. Conduct consultation activities
36. Compile & issue updated draft documents
37. Hold recommendations and formal decision meeting(s)
38. Ensure stakeholder consensus exists
39. Prepare and present formal findings
40. Obtain formal approvals; ensure monitoring plan in place
41. Finalize & issue final report; acknowledge contributions
42. Package and secure files for subsequent reference
43. Ensure orientation of change/ implementation team
44. Monitor results; record on master tracking sheet
45. Compile study close-out report; feed to corporate system.

14. Value and Risk Management

Applying a Combined Value & Risk Management Approach

Value and risk are inextricably linked. The traditional Value Methodology does not formally address risk. However, through its logical process and multi-stakeholder representation, a value study workshop is an ideal forum to identify and categorize project risks and uncertainties.

A consistent value and risk managed approach provides a basic framework and a tool-set to address issues of potential misunderstanding and misalignment at the start of a project, and in many cases, results in significant reductions in the whole life costs of the completed project. Outcomes are based on a common understanding of needs, constraints, key concerns, major risk areas, life cycle impacts and shared/negotiated team values.

Major projects require special consideration of risk and complexity in order to produce reasonable and manageable contingencies. Timeframes of large projects are typically long, thus leaving the potential for significant change in economic, political and physical conditions / requirements. Third-party requirements often have a high potential for change and hence risk. Assumptions, estimates and contingency allowances should be tracked and re-evaluated throughout the different stages of a project. *The risk management process is described in Reference 4.*

Risks (and value) can appear quite differently to clients, consultants, contractors, insurers and other stakeholders. Often a risk and value assessment becomes the basis for negotiations between impacted parties, which in turn may become the basis of obtaining the necessary approvals to proceed with the project. For example, negotiations may revolve around risk transfer, compensation, adequacy of environmental protection, etc. Objective and traceable assessment is therefore required to facilitate discussion between the various parties. The value and risk management (VRM) process is eminently suitable for this.

15. Summing Up

The value study approach may be applied to a wide range of small, complex projects through to large projects or programs. Early application as an integral component of the strategic procurement process leads to significant savings relating to schedule, staff time, capital costs and life-cycle costs. In addition, experience shows that 'it is never too late' to derive substantial benefits in terms of enhanced functionality, team building and cost improvement.

A value study is a time saving, cost effective, consensus and team building process. It is used to plan, develop and control projects, together with aiding transformation of business culture/practices and compatibility with community needs. Advanced value and risk management techniques applied through teams familiar with the process make for particularly quick and robust results. There are different value-based approaches, techniques and tools that are offered through various organizations, yielding results as diverse as the effort expended.

The key to proper time allocation for a value study is to demonstrate that enhancing value is not a "quick fix", but an integral part of the project initiation and continuing development process. By far the most suitable situation is for this management process to be introduced at the highest level in an organization. This normally requires it to be seen to be non-threatening and compatible with ongoing processes and for there to be little upheaval to daily routines. The function-based, value and risk study process is particularly effective when applied as both a:

> (i) program navigational tool, and,

> (ii) project/product/service improvement tool.

A value study is a very powerful, group thinking and consensus building process. The information in this booklet is necessarily brief. Additional techniques may be included at any stage. More information is available in the publications listed on **pages 38, 39**.

Appendix
Enhanced Value Study Considerations
Various Viewpoints

Around the world there are quite widely differing interpretations of what a value study is and what it can accomplish. Definitions of related terms such as value analysis (VA), value engineering (VE) and value management (VM) may be synonymous, or, somewhat different, depending on local jurisdictions and practices. It is noteworthy that there are many cases of very short, partial applications being promoted as *bone fide* VA, VE or VM. For some of those cases, results are sub optimal. Of course, partial applications may have validity. However, the results of shorter interventions are far more meaningful if anchored within a continuing framework focused on value improvement.

Value Methodology

The long established, Value Methodology is the process by which many formal value studies are conducted and is a very powerful means by which to establish best value solutions. The six phases of the Value Methodology workshop process (Information, Function Analysis, Creativity, Evaluation, Development and Presentation) form an excellent and easy-to-remember basic, guiding "road map". In practice there are many considerations and other activities required to conduct a cost-effective study, particularly for large, complex, multi-stakeholder programs and projects. As well, a more rigorous and comprehensive approach is required to ensure readiness for each step in a longer sequence of steps.

Expectations and Preparedness

There are widely differing interpretations of the time required to prepare for and conduct effective workshops and related follow-up. This can cause issues when specifying or responding to a request for service for a value study. During implementation of such a service, there can be a corresponding mismatch of various stakeholders' expectations, leading to a lack of recognition of all potential value improvement opportunities. It should be noted that the Value Methodology was originally intended for application over at least a 5-days (and sometimes 3-weeks) duration workshop and through a small team of (5 to 7) subject matter experts, participating on a full-time basis.

Enhanced Value Improvement Process

The enhanced value improvement process addresses the modern-day trend toward much shorter (1.5 to 2 days duration) workshops having large numbers of (say, 24 to 80) participants.

The foregoing sections 2 to 15 (pages 3 to 29) describe the process for an effective value study. Figures 3 and 4, (shown on pages 7 & 10 respectively), illustrate the enhanced, overall framework for conducting value studies. Phenomenal results are typically obtained through completion of the whole process. This may be done in one, hurried, continuous application or in a series of relatively leisurely applications that address the whole process.

The following illustrations build on this and describe four key study stages, plus a useful post study review of effectiveness:

❖ Establishing a Framework for Success (Study Start-up)

❖ Creating the Conditions for Success (Workshop Inputs)

❖ Exploring Possibilities for Value Improvement (Workshop)

❖ Ensuring Effective Outcomes (Workshop Follow-through)

and, optional,

❖ Post Study Review (Assessment of Study Effectiveness).

The stages include 23 steps and a total of 108 considerations / activities from the beginning to the end of the whole value study. The illustrations provide a comprehensive checklist for planning an effective value review. There are some activities shown that are additional to those required for a traditional Value Methodology study.

This enhanced process needs not be particularly lengthy; - it is just that the several steps and activities are identified explicitly (rather than assumed to be implicit). The enhanced value study process also greatly assists in preparing to conduct shorter workshops. In so doing, the study process can be paced to suit the needs and availability of the various stakeholder representatives.

Enhanced Value Study Considerations

Establishing a Framework for Success

Purpose: To Ensure Overall Understanding of Requirements & Timelines

Study Start-up

A. Initial Appreciation & Establishing Expectations

- ☐ Overall Strategic Aims, (Vision, Mission) and Justification (Why)
- ☐ Problem / Opportunity Statement, incl. Size of "Prize"
- ☐ Value Study Mandate
- ☐ Overall Scope; "Must Do" & "No-Go" Areas
- ☐ Key Result Areas

B. Initial Diagnostic Review

- ☐ Strategic FAST / FOCUS Diagram
- ☐ Business Case Parameters
- ☐ Condition Assessment
- ☐ Key Risk, Issues & Opportunity Areas
- ☐ Quantifiable Targets
- ☐ Value Drivers & Overall Performance Metrics
- ☐ Sources & Accuracy of Data Inputs
- ☐ Team Members
- ☐ External Specialists and Supports

C. Value Study Terms of Reference & Work Plan

- ☐ Study Purpose and Goals / Targets
- ☐ Study Scope & Exclusions
- ☐ Study Sponsor and Manager
- ☐ VM Process Steps
- ☐ Stakeholder Issues
- ☐ Level of Effort
- ☐ Resources
- ☐ Study Timings
- ☐ Workshop(s) Agenda
- ☐ Deliverables

D. Study Support Logistics

- ☐ Scheduling of Participants, Workshop and Meetings
- ☐ Contracts
- ☐ Venue & Equipment
- ☐ Joining Instructions & Expectations
- ☐ Site Visit Arrangements

Enhanced Value Study Considerations
(Continued)

Creating the Conditions for Success

Purpose: To Ensure Readiness to Proceed to Workshop(s)

Preparation of Workshop Input Package

E. Initial Orientation
- ☐ Planning Team VM Orientation
- ☐ VM Orientation for Other Interested Parties
- ☐ Questionnaire / Interviews with Key Personnel as Required

F. Program /Project Requirements
- ☐ Needs Definition and Areas of Concern
- ☐ Planning Envelope (e.g. Trends & Projections)
- ☐ Operating Extremes (e.g. demand, flow, temperature)
- ☐ Assumptions;
- ☐ Sensitivities
- ☐ Service Levels / Life
- ☐ Scope & Exclusions
- ☐ Interfaces &
- ☐ Interdependencies
- ☐ Screening Criteria
- ☐ Functional Perf. Spec.
- ☐ Special Considerations
- ☐ Budget & Timelines

G. Definition of Base Case
- ☐ Process & Layouts
- ☐ Design Premise
- ☐ Systems Overviews
- ☐ Capital and Life Cycle Costs
- ☐ Schedule
- ☐ Standards
- ☐ Benchmarking
- ☐ System Modeling
- ☐ Redundancies
- ☐ Contingencies

H. Assessment of Base Case Performance
- ☐ Function Analysis
- ☐ Function-Cost Models
- ☐ Energy Models
- ☐ Risk Evaluation
- ☐ Performance Profiles
- ☐ Multi –Attribute Value Index
- ☐ Value Gap & Unknowns

J. Workshop Input Package
- ☐ VM Process Briefing
- ☐ Presentation(s)
- ☐ Handout; Photographs
- ☐ Site Visits as Necessary

Enhanced Value Study Considerations
(Continued)

Exploring Possibilities for Improvement

Purpose: To Ensure Thoroughness & Testing of Ideas

Innovation Workshop Activities

K. Team Orientation
- ☐ Team Briefing
- ☐ Summary Information Presentations

M. Target Areas for Improvement

Review Analysis of:
- ☐ Function Cost-worth
- ☐ High Risk
- ☐ Performance Gaps
- ☐ Key Issues
- ☐ Excessive Cost Areas
- ☐ Schedule Concerns

N. Creativity
- ☐ Structured Creativity

P. Screening
- ☐ Screening, Extension & Initial Evaluation of Creative Ideas

Q. Development
- ☐ Testing & Outline Development of Ideas into Value Enhancement Proposals (VEPs)

R. Consolidation
- ☐ Collation and Comparison
- ☐ Formulation of Scenarios
- ☐ Life Cycle Implications
- ☐ Re-Assessment of Proposals; Trade-offs
- ☐ Risk Impacts & Mitigation
- ☐ Key Messages
- ☐ Update Function, Cost, Schedule, Risk, Performance Models and Value Index
- ☐ Management Action Plan
- ☐ Implementation Roadblocks
- ☐ Impacts on Other Areas
- ☐ Initial Read-out

Enhanced Value Study Considerations
(Continued)

Ensuring Effective Outcomes

Purpose: To Ensure Clarity of Proposals & Action Plan and Confirm Consensus

Post Workshop Follow-through

S Interim Outputs

- ☐ Assimilation of Feedback
- ☐ Fine-tuning of VEPs
- ☐ Collate Master Spreadsheet of Impacts
- ☐ Review, Select, Combine & Categorize VEPs
- ☐ Compile Interim Output Summary
- ☐ Encourage Additional Ideas
- ☐ Develop VEPs Summaries
- ☐ Review Risk Impacts & Risk Management Plan
- ☐ Complete Workshop Diary

T. Firming-up

- ☐ Confirm Technical & Financial Feasibility
- ☐ Prepare Draft Output Overview
- ☐ Complete Output Presentation
- ☐ Develop Recommendations
- ☐ Consult Stakeholders

U. Study Completion

- ☐ Consider Additional Ideas Submitted
- ☐ Update Layout & Systems Descriptions
- ☐ Develop Change Plan
- ☐ Develop Monitoring Plan
- ☐ Obtain Approvals
- ☐ Complete Final Output Report
- ☐ Formally Close Study

MONITORING & REPORTING of IMPLEMENTATION of VALUE ENHANCEMENT PROPOSALS / CHANGE (By Others)

Enhanced Value Study Considerations
(Continued)

Purpose: To Confirm Realization of Benefits & Improve Corporate Value Program

Post Study Review

Assessment of Study Effectiveness

V. Implementation Record of Value Enhancement Proposals & Monitoring Updates
- Predicted Value Improvement & Related Benefits
- Value Improvement Realized
- Updated Risk Management / Mitigation

W. Creation or Updating of Value File
- Stakeholder Requirements
- Key Value & Performance Criteria

X. Evaluation of Study Performance & Cost Effectiveness
- Critical Review of Study Outcomes
- Return on Study Effort

Y. Compilation of Lessons Learned
- Key Learnings
- Areas for Improvement in Other Applications

Z. Feedback to Value Improvement Program & Data Warehouse
- Updating of Value Improvement Program Results
- Essential Data Capture and Input to Corporate Data Base

About the Author

Martyn Phillips, FICE, FCIWEM, FSAVE, FHKIVM, CVS®, CVM, PVM, P.Eng.
Fellow, Institution of Civil Engineers (UK); Fellow, Chartered Institution of Water and Environmental Management (UK); Fellow, SAVE International (US); Fellow, Hong Kong Institute of Value Management; Certified Value Specialist –Life (US); Certificated Value Manager (UK); Professional in Value Management (EU), Professional Engineer (Canada)

Martyn Phillips is a seasoned value specialist with a strong background in both technical and program / project management. He has worked in several different countries and diverse cultures throughout the world. His leadership of opportunity and problem-solving explorations has resulted in substantial savings of time and capital (& life-cycle) cost, while maintaining quality.

This includes reduced risk and significant constructability / functionality / productivity enhancements, for many high profile, public and private sector programs, projects and services.

He is well qualified as both a Professional Engineer and a Value Specialist in Europe and in North America. He assists organizations achieve their business goals, particularly through planning & optimization of major initiatives. He is recognized as a world-class practitioner in value and performance improving practices and has served on various professional committees.

Martyn also conducts strategic and operational consulting assignments, as well as performance improvement training / coaching and change management for a wide range of clients and topics worldwide. His business activities also include organizational efficiencies and effectiveness, interim management, independent reviews, program / major project planning and controls, as well as project rescue, along with transformation of business processes.

Publications in This Series

"Closing the Performance Gap" Series on Achieving Best Value Programs, Projects, Products, Systems & Services:

Executive Focus

In Search of Value

Aligning the Road to High Performance

Ref.

1. **An Introduction to Value Assurance**
   ISBN 978-1480011953

2. **Overview,** *Closing the Performance Gap with Value Assurance*   ISBN 978-1477553831

Beginner * *& Practitioner Focus*

3. **Part 1, Managing Expectations:** *Understanding the Conditions for Success*   ISBN 978-1468168150

4. **Part 2, Methods:** *Assuring Best Value and Managing Uncertainty*   ISBN 978-1468168198

Value Solutions

Creating and Delivering Better Solutions in Less Time

5. **An Introduction to Conducting Value Studies** *
   ISBN 978-0991737864

6. **Value Methodology Fundamentals***
   Application Guide
   ISBN 978-1477581032

7. **Managing Value Management**
   Intermediate VM Training Guide
   ISBN 978-1477673751

Further information may be obtained from:

info@valueassurance.org

Other Publications & Standards

Some relevant publications are listed below. Readers should check on the appropriate internet websites for the latest updates.

Value Methodology Standard, March 2015, SAVE International

Function Analysis Guide, 2016, SAVE International,

Certification Examination Study Guide, September 1st, 2011, SAVE International

Certification Program Manual, 13th Edition January 9th, 2015 SAVE International

Value Methodology: A Pocket Guide to Reduce Cost and Improve Value Through Function Analysis, Miles Value Foundation/GOAL/QPC, 2008

BS EN 12973:2000, Value Management Guidelines to Its Use and Intent, Institute of Value Management / British Standards Institute/ IVM

An Executive Guide to Value Management, 2010, Office of Government Commerce

Life Cycle Costing for Design Professionals, 2nd Edition, 1995. Dr. Stephen J. Kirk, Alphonse J. Dell'Isola.

Techniques of Value Analysis and Engineering, 1990. 3rd Edition, Miles, Lawrence D. / Miles Value Foundation

Value Management, 1988. Kaufman, Jerry J.

Selected Papers/Presentations

Third Party Value, Julia S. Dale, SAVE Conference Proceedings, 1995

Value Improvement for the 21st Century, Ginger Adams, Value World (SAVE International), Volume No. 19, Number 1, March 1996

A Value and Risk Management Approach to Project Development, Martyn R. Phillips, Proceedings of the Institution of Civil Engineers, May 2002, Volume 150, Issue 2.

Price is what you pay. Value is what you get.

Source: Warren Buffet

My model for business is The Beatles. They were four guys who kept each other's kind of negative tendencies in check. They balanced each other and the total was greater than the sum of the parts. That's how I see business; great things in business are never done by one person, they're done by a team of people.

Source: Steve Jobs

www.ingramcontent.com/pod-product-compliance
Lightning Source LLC
Chambersburg PA
CBHW041715200326

41519CB00001B/170